Heads Up

The Story of One Quarter

Molly Schaar Idle

Abingdon Press

Nashville

Heads Up

The Story of One Quarter

Requests for permission should be submitted in writing to:
Abingdon Press, 201 Eighth Avenue South, Nashville, TN 37203,
faxed to (615) 749-6128, or submitted via email to *permission@abingdonpress.com*.

Scripture quotation is from the New Revised Standard Version of the Bible.
Copyright © 1989 by the Division of Christian Education of the National Council of Churches of Christ in the U.S.A.
Used by permission.

ISBN 0-687-34213-9

04 05 06 07 08 09 10 11 12 13 – 10 9 8 7 6 5 4 3 2 1

Printed in China

To Mom and Dad.

The richest people I know.

One day the house was full.

And the next...

Mom and Dad's store had closed,
and everything they owned was gone.

Consequently,
Agnes sat moping in a corner.

"Time to go, Aggie," Dad called from the doorway.

"It's not fair," muttered Agnes. "Maybe not," said Dad, "but sometimes bad things happen to good people."

"Have faith," he said scooping her up. "We still have the most important thing of all!"

"What's that?"

"We have each other," answered Mom from the hall. "And we have God looking out for us. That calls for a three-way snuggle!"

That doesn't seem like so very much, thought Agnes, sulking as she was wrapped in her parents' arms.

She wanted her toys, her dolls, her books, her room! But they were all gone. Now they had to move and live with Manna and Papa until times were better.

As they put on their coats to leave, Dad reached into his pocket, looking for his keys and found instead... a single quarter.

"That's a good sign," he grinned. "Now we always have a way to call home if we need one another in an emergency."

And when they arrived at Manna and Papa's, Dad placed the quarter atop the dresser in the room that the three of them would share. Every day Mom and Dad took turns looking for work.

Every day the one who went out took the quarter.

And some days,
     Agnes went too.

Walking down near the beach, she and Dad passed the boardwalk. There were games to play, ice cream to eat, and...a Ferris wheel to ride!

"Dad, may I ride it?" pleaded Agnes.

"No, Aggie. I'm sorry, but we don't have the money."

"You have the quarter in your pocket!" pointed out Agnes.

"But that is just in case of emergencies—in case we need each other."

Agnes furrowed her brow and kicked at the sand.

"But..." said Dad,

"…I do know a ride that's free."

14

15

Another day, Agnes and Mom were
out walking and got caught in the rain.
Hiding under a tree, Agnes squealed,
"Let's use the quarter and call Dad
to come get us!"

"I'm not sure this is an emergency," said Mom, smiling mischievously. "But…"

"...It could definitely be fun!"

19

But a day came when Agnes was out with Mom and Dad (and the quarter) that no distraction would appease her.

They passed a shop in town, and in the window was the most beautiful doll Agnes had ever seen.

It cost more than a quarter, to be sure. Agnes' face burned when she thought of how much she wanted it. And even though she knew they could not afford to buy it, she lingered a long time in front of the shop.

Mom and Dad must have noticed because a couple of days later Agnes found a doll sitting on her pillow. Not the one from the shop window, but one her Mom had made from fabric scraps and mismatched buttons found around the house. Agnes surveyed it, and her face did nothing to hide her disappointment.

"Do you like her?" asked Mom hopefully.

Agnes shrugged as she held up the doll. "She's not like the one in the shop," said Agnes, setting the doll on the dresser. Mom looked hurt but said nothing.

That night, after saying her prayers, Agnes overheard Mom and Dad talking in whispers on the stairs.

"Maybe it's not fair to Aggie," she heard Mom's voice say softly. "Maybe being together isn't enough."

"Would it be better if I left to take a job out of town?" wondered Dad aloud. "Then she could have more of the things we wish we could give her."

Agnes looked again at the handmade doll atop the dresser next to the single quarter and turned over in bed.

Dad gone?

She hadn't meant for anything like that to happen.
Her face burned again, not from want this time, but
from shame. She closed her eyes, but for a long time she
could not fall asleep.

When she woke up the next
morning and looked at the dresser, the rag
doll was there; but the quarter was gone. She raced
downstairs to the kitchen and found Mom at the
table, but Dad was nowhere to be seen.

"Where's Dad?"

"He left an hour ago, sweetheart," said Mom from
behind the newspaper.

"He's gone? But I need to talk to him. It's an
emergency!"

"What is it?" asked Mom, drawing her close.

Agnes' eyes filled with tears as she said, "Oh, Mom, I didn't mean for Dad to go away! No doll, no anything is worth that! Nothing is more important than being together! I need to tell Dad."

"And you just did," said a voice from the doorway.

There was Dad, beaming at the two of them.

"You are so right, Aggie. Being together is the most important thing of all," he said, scooping her into his arms. "But there are other good things too, such as celebrating my new job with ice cream sundaes!"

29

"This calls for a three-way snuggle!" exclaimed Agnes.

And snuggled in between Mom and Dad at the soda fountain, she grinned, thanking God that they were together. She knew she wouldn't trade this moment for all the quarters in the world.

31

"Love one another."
(John 15:12)

The End.